WORLD MYTHS AND LEGENDS II

Southeast Asia

Gus Gedatus

Fearon/Janus/Quercus
Belmont, CA
Simon & Schuster Education Group

World Myths and Legends

Greek and Roman
Ancient Middle Eastern
Norse
African
Far Eastern
Celtic
Native American
Regional American

HISTORY
AND
CULTURE

World Myths and Legends II

India
Russia
Europe
South America
The Caribbean
Central America
Mexico
Southeast Asia

Series Editor: Joseph T. Curran
Cover Designer: Dianne Platner
Text Designer: Teresa A. Holden
Interior Illustrations: Mary Beth Gaitskill
Cover Photo: The Granger Collection, New York

Library of Congress Catalog Card Number: 92–72300
ISBN 0–8224–4631–6
Printed in the United States of America
2. 10 9 8 7 6 5 4 3 2
EB

CONTENTS

An Introduction to the Myths and Legends of Southeast Asia

This book contains folk legends from these countries in Southeast Asia: Vietnam, Laos, Malaysia, Thailand, Cambodia, Indonesia, Singapore, and the Philippines. Many of these stories focus on the earth, the weather, and other elements of nature. Throughout history, Southeast Asians have been very curious about the physical world around them. As you may wonder about the planets or the causes of storms, so did the early Southeast Asians. Many of their legends are explanations of how the earth began and why certain natural events occur.

Some legends explain the origin of volcanoes or earthquakes. Because many Southeast Asians live close to the seas, they have told tales about strange creatures who lived there.

Many Southeast Asian legends tell stories with simple moral lessons that people need to know. These lessons help people live in harmony with one another and with nature. Also, some Southeast Asian legends tell stories of strong and powerful women as well as strong and powerful men.

Some Southeast Asian myths tell about amazing powers possessed by people. Some heroes change their shapes. Other characters come upon objects that have magical powers. These things, such as a special gem or a weapon, help the heroes get out of trouble.

Animals are very popular in Southeast Asian legends. Some of the animals are quite ordinary. Others talk like humans or have special powers and abilities. In this book, you will read stories about a snake, a buffalo, a turtle, a tiger, and a butterfly. Legends such as these show that people have both feared and admired animals and have told stories based on these feelings.

The Sea Dragon and the Fairy Queen

This legend comes from Vietnam. It tells the story of how people were created by the uniting of the land and the sea.

Once a great mist swirled over the earth. Mountains, meadows, forests, oceans, and all the things of nature were very quiet and peaceful.

Then the ocean began to rumble. Waves crashed against the shore. The Sea Dragon appeared from out of the bubbling foam.

This creature stood taller than the highest mountain. He had long, sharp claws and a wide, powerful tail. His whole body was covered with shiny bronze scales. The Sea Dragon was the ruler of the sea.

At about the same time, the Fairy Queen appeared on the top of the highest mountain. She was the ruler of the land.

When the Fairy Queen walked from mountaintop to mountaintop, the wind danced around her. Every time she opened her mouth to speak, a lovely tune came out.

When the Sea Dragon saw the Fairy Queen on top of the mountain, he stood very still. Then the waters of the sea became as smooth as glass. The Fairy Queen stood still, too, and she quieted her singing.

"Dear Fairy Queen," said the great dragon, "you have a great beauty and majesty. It is unlike any I have ever seen in the ocean."

"Sea Dragon, you have such great strength and power," the Fairy Queen said. "With you to protect me, I would never fear for the safety of my land."

The Fairy Queen extended her dainty hand toward the sea. The Sea Dragon reached toward her. Their touch united the land and the sea forever. The love of the two rulers bonded their power and majesty.

Many days and nights passed as the waters and the land grew stronger and more beautiful. Then one day, the seas surged with pride, and the winds sang with joy. The Fairy Queen was about to give birth.

The Sea Dragon, happy about the birth, clapped his tail against the shore. He swam and dived in the seas to show his joy.

A grand hush fell over all the land and sea. Then a bright light shone down from the heavens. The Fairy Queen laid one hundred eggs on the seashore. Soon beautiful sons and daughters sprang from the pearly eggs.

The Sea Dragon and the Fairy Queen cared for their one hundred children until they were fully grown.

Then the Fairy Queen took fifty of their children and traveled high into the mountains. There these sons and daughters became hunters and highland farmers.

The Sea Dragon took the other fifty children to the sea. There they became Vietnam's first fishers and farmers of the lower seacoast.

The Sea Dragon called upon the firstborn of the one hundred children for a special task. This strong young man was named Hung Vuong. His task was to become the first ruler of the people of Vietnam. The Hung Vuong Dynasty lasted from 2879 B.C. to 258 B.C.

1. *Over what did the Fairy Queen rule?*
2. *What happened when the Sea Dragon and the Fairy Queen first saw each other?*
3. *What became of the one hundred children born to the Sea Dragon and the Fairy Queen?*

The Fisher's Daughter

Many people fear swimming in the waters of the beautiful Lingayen Gulf of the Philippines. This legend tells why the god of the gulf occasionally takes someone, usually a child, to his underworld kingdom.

Many years ago, a fisher and his wife had a beautiful little girl. The girl was so cheerful that the couple named her Maliket, which means "happy."

As Maliket grew, she became smart and very strong. She liked cooking for her parents, cleaning their house, and doing whatever they asked.

Maliket's favorite sport was riding in a little *banca*, or boat, that her father had built for her. She spent many afternoons paddling through canals and exploring hidden coves in the waters near her home.

One afternoon Maliket came home with bunches of colorful weeds piled in the back of her banca.

"Where did you get these strange weeds?" her father asked.

"I found them when I went swimming in a

4

cove at the foot of the mountain," Maliket said. She pointed to a far-off mountain peak.

"That is a very dangerous place, my child," warned her father. "That is where Maksil, the god of this gulf, takes his daily nap. I have heard that he will punish anyone who disturbs him there. You must promise me that you will never go back again."

"It is a very beautiful place, Father," the girl replied. "However, I will still obey you and not go there again."

It so happened that the god Maksil had seen Maliket swimming in his cove. He decided that he wanted the girl to become his daughter. She would take the place of his child who had died a few years before. Maksil's servant, Giant Squid, had promised to watch for Maliket and to guide her banca back to Maksil.

The following day Maliket took her banca out once again. She felt the boat being pulled toward that same cove. Maliket didn't want to break her promise to her father. She tried to paddle the other way, but the boat continued toward the cove.

Maliket's banca was drawn into the cove. Then it was pulled down into the water. Maliket found herself in a tunnel. She was afraid until she began to look at all of the wonderful things around her. Many colorful flowers lined the sides of the tunnel. Maliket saw strange-looking fish. She heard the fish talking and laughing as they saw her coming. Oddly enough, she could understand every sound they made.

"Welcome, Maliket! Welcome, new daughter!" the fish cried out.

All of a sudden, Maliket heard a loud clap, like the slamming of a very heavy door. All the fish swam away. Maliket's banca suddenly hit a sandy shore. She flew out of the little boat onto a bed of green moss.

Maliket looked up at a tall golden creature sitting in a high-backed chair. He was half human and half fish. He was wearing a glittering crown and holding a silver staff shaped like a huge eel.

"Don't be afraid," the creature said to the trembling girl. "I am Maksil, the god of the gulf. I have brought you here to be my new daughter. I will give you everything I can to make you happy."

"I can't stay here," Maliket replied sadly. "I want to go home. My dear parents will miss me."

"Ah, but you must stay!" Maksil

Maksil, god of the gulf

commanded. He could see how the little girl was shaking with fear, so he spoke more kindly.

"Soon you will become happy here," Maksil said. "Then you will forget about your home." He used his staff to point to a palace glistening with diamonds.

"That shining palace will be your home from now on," the god continued. "You will have fine clothes and toys and as many playmates as you wish. Now come with me."

Maksil offered Maliket his giant hand, but she didn't want to go with him. So Maksil called for his guards, who carried Maliket off to the palace.

In the palace, mermaids gathered to bathe Maliket and to dress her in a flowing silver dress. One mermaid put a crown of pearls on her head. Another brought her a box of the loveliest jewels in the undersea kingdom. None of these things made Maliket feel any better.

"Please tell your master that I just want to go home," she cried to the mermaids. "My old parents need me to help them."

The god of the gulf brought in clowns and magicians, hoping that they would make Maliket smile. Little boys and girls, all half human and half fish, taught her to play games. Maliket did smile a little but never for very long.

Maksil thought that Maliket was starting to like her new home. However, he was very wrong about this.

One day Maliket found a magic mirror on a shelf in her room. When Maliket looked into the mirror, she could see her parents. They were both growing ill with the sadness of having lost their little girl. This made Maliket cry harder than ever before. Akulaw, the woman who took care of Maliket, felt sorry for her.

"You do so want to go home, don't you, my dear?" Akulaw asked.

"Oh, yes, I do," Maliket said.

"I was brought here years ago, too, so I know how you feel," Akulaw said. "Now I am an old woman, and my family is long gone."

"Please help me get away from here," Maliket begged. "You can come with me!"

"No, I am too old to leave," Akulaw replied, "but I will help you escape."

That same night Akulaw put a sleeping powder into Giant Squid's drink. Instead of guarding the palace, Giant Squid fell asleep. Then Akulaw took Maliket to the place where her banca lay hidden. Akulaw and one of her friends led Maliket's banca back to the seawaters.

Maksil always tucked Maliket into bed each night. This night he found that she was gone. He awakened Giant Squid and sent him after Maliket. However, Giant Squid, still drowsy from the sleeping powder, didn't move very quickly.

As Maliket was paddling her banca in the open sea toward her parent's home, she saw Giant Squid. He was swimming closer and closer to her. As her banca neared the shore, her father and some of his friends heard her shouting for help. Giant Squid reached a long arm into the banca. Just then Maliket's father pulled her to safety in his own boat. His friends beat Giant Squid with long paddles. Finally the great creature gave up and returned to the undersea kingdom.

Maksil was angry. He forced Giant Squid to go back to the cove at least one time every year. Each time that Giant Squid returns to the cove, he twirls his many arms beneath the waters. Then he pulls another child down to the kingdom of Maksil, god of the gulf.

1. *Why did Maliket go back to the cove after her father had asked her not to?*

2. *Why didn't Maliket want to stay in Maksil's kingdom?*

3. *Who was Akulaw?*

Why the Monsoon Comes Every Year

In Vietnam, a yearly monsoon brings violent winds and heavy rain. To explain this event, this story gives voices and feelings to the elements of nature.

Princess Mi Nuong was beautiful but also very sad. Lately she had begun to see wrinkles on her face when she looked in the mirror.

Over the years, many men had wanted to marry the Princess. Not one of them, however, had pleased her father, the emperor. It was a custom of the time for a daughter not to marry unless her father approved.

Princess Mi Nuong was the emperor's only child. The emperor wanted to be sure that she married a man who was both rich and powerful. The Princess, however, began to think that she would never marry.

One day two men appeared at the same time, both wanting to see Princess Mi Nuong. One man was called the Power of the Sea, the other was the Power of the Mountains.

The emperor liked both men very much,

so he could not choose one over the other. Finally he told them, "Whoever is the first to bring gifts to my daughter will become her husband."

The Power of the Sea called his many men together and had them search the sea for treasures. They helped him gather thousands of gleaming pearls, tender squid, and juicy crabs.

The Power of the Mountains called his men together, too. They gathered rare mountain fruits. The Power of the Mountains opened his magic wish book. Using the wish book, he filled a chest with priceless emeralds and diamonds.

The Power of the Mountains arrived at the emperor's palace as the sun was rising one morning. The emperor was impressed with the precious gems. As he had promised, he allowed his daughter to marry the Power of the Mountains. The emperor gave his daughter and her husband-to-be a splendid wedding celebration. Then the smiling Princess left the palace with her new husband.

Shortly after, the Power of the Sea arrived at the palace. He had brought several dozen men, all carrying trays piled

The Power of the Mountains brings gifts

high with seafood and beautiful pearls.

The Power of the Sea found out that the Power of the Mountains had reached the palace first. The Power of the Sea was angry because he had lost the Princess. He told his men to go after the Power of the Mountains and bring Mi Nuong back to him.

From that moment on, the Power of the Sea brought winds to blow and rains to fall. The ocean rose higher and higher. Giant waves rushed over the land.

All the sea creatures became soldiers of the Power of the Sea. They chased after the Power of the Mountains and his bride. Wherever they ran, rivers flooded and people were killed.

The Power of the Sea and his soldiers were getting near the Power of the Mountains. The ocean waves destroyed more and more crops and homes. More and more people were killed.

The people prayed that the Power of the Sea and the Power of the Mountains would end their fighting. However, for many more days and nights, the battle continued.

Finally the Power of the Mountains remembered his magic wish book. He opened it and asked that his mountain grow higher and higher. The mountain grew. Then the Power of the Mountains took the Princess to the highest peak. They were well out of the reach of the Power of the Sea.

The Power of the Sea realized that further battle was pointless. So he marched his men back to the sea. The floods stopped. The Power of the Sea was still angry.

So it is that every year the Power of the Sea sends rushing waters and strong winds onto the land. Even today the Power of the Sea hopes that he can get back the Princess Mi Nuong for his own bride. For this reason, the monsoon comes each year to Vietnam.

1. *What kind of man did the emperor want his daughter to marry?*
2. *How did the Power of the Mountains collect all the diamonds and emeralds to give to the Princess?*
3. *How did the Power of the Sea continue to try to get Princess Mi Nuong for his bride?*

The Tale of Tao

In the mythology of the Philippines, life began with Tao. This is the story of that beginning.

Many thousands of years ago, Sky was so close to Earth that they almost touched each other. During this time, only one man lived on Earth. His name was Tao.

Tao was very good friends with Sky and Earth. Each day the three of them talked about the wonders of the world. Tao had a guitar that he played every evening to amuse his friends. He also had a large mortar and pestle. He used this bowl and tool to grind rice into flour for his food.

When Tao first came to Earth, he had built a little hut from palm leaves. Tao had a few treasures. He had two lamps, which he kept beside his hut. One was Moon. The other was Sun. Tao also had Star Belt, a band of a thousand stars.

Before going to bed each night, Tao hung Moon in Sky. Then he talked with his friends.

"Dear Sky," Tao said, "how beautiful you look with the glow of Moon on you."

"Yes, thank you, Tao," Sky replied. "Look at the way Moon's light also makes Earth shine."

Then Earth had to speak up, too. "How handsome you are, Tao, with the Moon's light on your face."

Then Earth, Sky, and Tao sang together as Tao strummed his guitar.

Before Tao went to sleep, he wrapped Star Belt around his waist. Sometimes Tao wandered in his sleep. Star Belt helped guide him back.

In the morning, Tao took Moon from Sky and returned it to the side of his little hut. Then he hung Sun in Moon's place.

"Good Earth," Tao said, "how lovely the warm, yellow light of Sun makes you look today."

"Yes, I know," Earth said, "and Sky glows so clearly with Sun's bright rays."

Then Sky had to speak up, too.

"Dear Tao," said Sky, "Sun's light casts the finest glow on your own face."

Then the three friends sang together again. Since it was now day, they sang the praises of Sun.

When the friends had finished singing, Tao went about his daily work. During the rainy months, Tao would sow rice in his fields. In the dry season, he would harvest the rice and pound it into flour with his mortar and pestle.

Life continued this way for a long time. The friends talked and sang. Tao planted crops for his food. However, one day the three friends had a terrible fight.

Tao had grown weary and sore from pounding rice with his mortar and pestle.

"I'm sure getting tired of this hard work," Tao said.

"Why are you complaining?" Earth asked. "You want to eat, don't you?"

"After all," Sun added, "that's the only work you have to do. The gods take care of everything else. They give you fruit and water and fish from the sea. Most of all, they make your rice grow very well."

Tao was getting angry. His arms kept going up and down. "Thud! Thud!" went the pestle as Tao beat it against the mortar.

"I hate this!" Tao yelled.

"You had better stop whining, or I'll send for the storm winds," Sky warned.

"I'll make the land shake and the rivers dry up!" Earth added.

Tao got angrier and angrier. Then he

Tao with his mortar and pestle

pounded harder and harder.

"I don't care what you do, Earth," Tao shouted. "Dry up all the rivers and make the land shake. Sky, send the storm winds if you must!"

Tao raised his pestle higher and pounded harder and harder. Each time he pounded, his pestle pushed Sky up and Earth down.

"Stop it!" Sky screamed. "You're pushing me away."

"That's right, stop it!" Earth yelled. "You're pushing me farther and farther down all the time."

"Well, if you don't stop yelling at me," Tao replied angrily, "I'll never stop pounding." The harder Tao pounded, the angrier he became.

Then Tao went to the side of his hut. He picked up Moon and hurled it into the air at Sun. He grabbed Star Belt and threw it high into Sky, too.

Day and night soon became confused. Sun, Moon, and Star Belt all glowed at the same time.

Tao was sorry for what he had done, but he didn't tell Earth and Sky. He was too proud to say anything. Instead, he went back to pounding his rice.

From that day on, Sky was so far away that Tao could no longer reach it. Earth was so low that he could no longer talk to Sky. The three friends knew that now the world had become a very different place for them.

In time, Sun once again shone only during the day, and Moon came out only at night.

Tao was sorry that he had lost his good friends. Sky was too far away to talk to him. Earth was too angry to speak to him ever again. Tao never got his treasures back. His two lamps, Sun and Moon, stayed in the sky. Star Belt stayed there, too.

The only things that Tao had left were his guitar and his mortar and pestle.

In the daytime in the Philippines, some people can still hear the thud of Tao's mortar and pestle.

1. *What two lamps did Tao keep beside his hut?*
2. *What did Tao wrap around his waist at night?*
3. *How did Sky get pushed so far upward?*

The Goddess in the Stalk of Rice

This Indonesian legend tells about what happened to an unhappy goddess when she went against her father's wishes.

The goddess Tisna Wati lived in heaven with her father, the god Batara Guru. Tisna Wati wasn't happy living in heaven. Most days she would look down on Earth, wishing that she were human.

Whenever her father came back from battling the demons against heaven, the princess would complain and cry.

"I'm getting tired of your complaints," her father said. "I wish I could send you down to Earth where you could live as a human. However, you have drunk of the magical life water, so you must remain a goddess forever. Soon I will choose the son of a god to be your husband."

Tisna Wati didn't want to marry the son of a god.

"Father," she replied, "I already know the man I will marry."

"Oh, really?" her father answered. "Who might that be?"

23

"He is not the son of a god," Tisna Wati said. "He lives on Earth. If you look down, you can see him working in his rice field."

"He is a human," her father replied, seeing the young man below. "You can't marry him. You are the daughter of a god. I will never let you marry him."

"Just wait and see," the daughter answered. "I will do as I please."

"I'd sooner change you into a stalk of rice," Tisna Wati's father warned. "I will choose a husband for you, and he will come from the sons of the gods."

Tisna Wati knew that she would never marry the son of a god.

The next day Batara Guru planned to search for a godly husband for his daughter. However, as he was about to leave, he received word of a new battle.

"I will fight this battle," he told his daughter. "When I come back, I will bring with me the man who will be your husband."

As soon as Batara Guru left, Tisna Wati called for the winds. She asked them to carry her down to Earth. She went to where the young human worked in his rice field on the side of the hill. As she watched the man, she knew now, more than ever, that he was the man she wanted to marry.

When the young man turned his plow up the hill, he saw Tisna Wati.

"What do you seek, lovely maid?" the young man asked.

"I seek my husband," she replied. "I think I have found him."

This pleased the young man, and he started laughing. Then Tisna Wati laughed, too. They laughed with the joy of two people in love. The sound was so loud that it traveled all the way up to heaven.

Batara Guru, deep in fierce battle against the demons, heard the loud laughter. He recognized his daughter's voice. Without a moment's pause, the angry father left the battle and rode the winds down to Earth. Soon he reached his daughter sitting beside the young man.

"Come with me, daughter," the god commanded. "I'm taking you back to heaven where you belong."

"Never!" Tisna Wati replied. "I want to stay here on Earth with my beloved."

"Is that so?" Batara Guru asked. "Then stay you will but not as the daughter of a god. You shall become a stalk of rice!"

At that instant, Tisna Wati turned into a

thin stalk of rice. She leaned toward the young man she loved. The young man sadly watched the lovely stalk. Then he touched it with his fingers.

Batara Guru felt very sad when he saw this gentle love before him.

"I was wrong," the god said. "I should have left them together. Now my daughter must remain a stalk of rice forever."

Suddenly Batara Guru had an idea. He changed the young man into a stalk of rice, too. In the breeze, the two stalks of rice swayed and bent together.

Since that time, people have heard the whispers of love of the rice stalks as they are carried on the soft mountain winds.

1. *Why did Batara Guru say Tisna Wati could not marry a human?*
2. *How did Tisna Wati get down to Earth?*
3. *Why did Batara Guru change his daughter into a stalk of rice?*

Why There Are No Tigers in Borneo

On most of the islands of Indonesia, such as Java and Sumatra, there are many tigers. On Borneo, however, there are none. This story tells why.

Many years ago, in the jungles of Java, the king of the tigers had no food. His followers were starving, and he himself would soon starve, too. The king sent a messenger to Borneo to tell its animals that they had to send food to Java. The messenger was unable to find the king of Borneo, but he did meet a tiny deer.

"I have a message for your king," the tiger roared. "He must surrender your land and all your food to the tigers of Java. If not, our king will bring great armies and destroy your kingdom."

"If you rest here," the little deer replied, "I will take that message to our king."

"Very well, but hurry," the tiger said. "Also give him this." The tiger gave the deer a tiger's whisker. "This whisker comes from the face of our great king. It shows how strong a king he is."

The deer took a long look at the whisker. "It is very large," the deer said. "He must be a powerful king."

"Be off with you," the tiger roared.

The deer bounded away to find his king.

"If those tigers from Java want food, they must want me!" the little deer thought as he ran. "I'm the perfect tiger food. I must think of something to do!" The deer ran until be met his friend the porcupine.

"Hey, what's your rush, little deer?" the porcupine asked.

"I'll tell you later, my friend," the deer replied. Then he got an idea. "Give me one of your quills," he said to the porcupine.

The porcupine pulled out one long stiff quill and gave it to the deer.

"You are a very good friend, porcupine," the deer said. "You have saved my life." Then the deer rushed off, leaving the porcupine a bit confused. The deer ran quickly back to the place where he had left the tiger.

"What took you so long?" the tiger yelled. "I haven't got all day!"

"I had to find our king," the deer explained. "Then I had to wait to see him."

"Did you give him my message?" the tiger asked.

"Oh, yes," the deer replied. "He said that he would welcome your king and his army. We haven't had a good fight here in Borneo for a very long time."

"What?" the tiger asked. "Did you show him the whisker from the face of our king?"

"Yes, I did, and he sent this one in return," the deer said. He handed the tiger the porcupine quill.

"This whisker came from the face of your king?" the tiger asked, quite stunned.

"Yes," the deer nodded.

"I will take it back to my country with the message from your king," the tiger said. The little deer smiled as the tiger left to hurry across land and sea to his home.

When the tiger got back to Java, he went straight to the king of tigers.

"Well, my servant, did you give my message to the ruler of Borneo?" the king asked.

"Yes, sir, I did," the tiger replied. "Their ruler sends word that he welcomes a battle with our armies."

"He's not afraid of the tigers of Java?" the king asked.

"No," the tiger replied. "He sends you this whisker from his own royal face." The

The deer presents the quill

messenger handed his king the quill from the porcupine. The king took a long look at the strong pointed whisker. Then he felt the whiskers on his own face.

"Perhaps we would be wiser to demand food of the elephants of Sumatra," the king decided.

No one is sure if the elephants of Sumatra ever sent food to the tigers of Java. However, to this day, no tigers can be found in Borneo.

1. *Why did the tiger king of Java send a messenger to Borneo?*
2. *Why was the deer afraid?*
3. *What did the deer give the messenger tiger to take to his king?*

Why the Hill Is Red

There is a hill in Singapore known to people as Red Hill. Some of the old people in that country still tell this story of how the hill got its name.

Many years ago, the waters around Singapore were filled with swordfish. People could not swim there because the swordfish would attack them. Fishers worked in constant danger of having their nets torn and their boats destroyed by the fierce fish.

One day the king, or rajah, of Singapore ordered his soldiers to form a line along the shore. The king ordered the men to spear the swordfish as the tide came in. However, the soldiers didn't have time to raise their spears. The swordfish rushed at the men, piercing them with their sharp swords.

The rajah then ordered a new line of men to take the soldiers' places. The fish killed these men, too. This happened again and again.

A young boy who was very saddened by all the killing went to speak with the rajah.

"Your Majesty," the boy said, "how can

you let all these soldiers be killed?"

"I don't know what else to do," the rajah replied. "The fish have to be stopped."

"Why don't you put a line of logs all along the beach?" the boy asked. "The logs can stop the fish."

The rajah was angry at first because this boy had tried to tell him how to protect his country. Then, after thinking about it, he decided the boy's idea might be a good one.

The rajah ordered his men to cut down hundreds of nearby trees. The soldiers then built a high wall along the shoreline with the logs. Then they waited for the tide.

Soon the tide brought thousands of swordfish to the shore. Their long swords easily pierced the wood of the logs. Then, however, the fish became stuck in those logs!

The soldiers moved in with their spears and killed every fish that was stuck in the logs. The next day more swordfish kept getting stuck, and the soldiers kept destroying them. Finally, after several days, there were no more swordfish left in the water.

The rajah was happy to learn that his people were at last safe from the swordfish. He was pleased with the cleverness of the

The swordfish of Singapore

boy, yet he was also worried. The rajah was afraid that such a wise person might grow up to take away his throne.

The rajah told his captain about his fears of the clever boy. The captain wanted to help the rajah. So he found the little boy's hut and killed him.

The little boy's blood ran down the hill and covered the shore. To this day, the hill has remained red. People are still sad because this young hero had been killed by the king's captain.

1. *How had the swordfish harmed the people?*
2. *Why did the young boy ask the rajah to consider a different way of destroying the swordfish?*
3. *Why was the rajah worried about the young boy?*

The Battle of the Buffalo

The roofs of many houses in western Sumatra have curved ends that look like the horns of buffalo. This story tells why the roofs are built this way.

An ancient rajah of the island of Java was so powerful that he had conquered many lands. Only a small part of western Sumatra, an island near Java, had not come under his rule. One day the rajah sent a messenger to the people of western Sumatra. His message told them that they had to surrender their lands to the rajah or be killed.

The people of western Sumatra gathered to discuss the rajah's message.

"We will not be able to win a battle against this powerful rajah," one man said. "He has fine weapons and an army of many thousands of men. We have old weapons and a small army."

"I think we must fight," another man said, "or we will be killed."

"If we do fight," a third man said, "many of us will die anyway."

"We have so few men and such old

weapons," one old man said. "So we must be very strong of mind. This demands some very serious thinking!"

The men of western Sumatra gathered together. They sat in a large circle and began to think. How could they save themselves and their families? What could they do to outsmart the rajah of Java?

At last the old man spoke up.

"I have an idea!" he said. "I know how we can save ourselves and our land."

"How? Tell us," the others eagerly responded.

"We must send a message to the rajah," the old man said. "It will remind him that in a fight many men on both sides will die. We can ask to send a buffalo into battle against one of the rajah's buffalo. We can say that if our buffalo wins, we will be free forever. If his wins, then we will all become the rajah's slaves."

"Where could we find a buffalo that would be sure to win?" one man asked. "If ours did not win, things would be as bad as if we had fought and lost."

"Then we must think some more," the old man replied to the rest of the people.

No one, however, could think of a better

plan. The people decided to try the plan. They would send the message to the rajah of Java. The people of western Sumatra chose a messenger to go to the rajah.

After weeks of travel, the messenger arrived at the rajah's palace. The messenger told the rajah of the people's plan to have two buffalo fight instead of two armies.

"Your Highness," the messenger said, "the people of western Sumatra will not surrender. Think about our plan. Would you rather see one buffalo die, or would you rather see many men die?"

The rajah thought for a moment about the people's plan.

"I do not wish to see any more bloodshed," the rajah replied. "I am determined, though, to make western Sumatra a part of my kingdom. Maybe your plan will work. All right! I will send the strongest buffalo in my lands to fight your people's buffalo."

Then the rajah laughed. "Think about this," he said. "Where will your people ever find a buffalo that can stand against mine? I have all of my many lands in which to find him. You have only the tiny area of western Sumatra."

While the rajah laughed, the messenger

left and returned to his people.

The people of western Sumatra were happy when they heard the messenger's news. Now they would not have to go to war.

The rajah prepared for the contest by sending his hunters across his hundreds of great prairies. They searched for the strongest buffalo. After only a few days, they returned with a huge, fierce, snorting buffalo. The rajah felt sure that the Sumatran buffalo would have no chance in a battle against this great beast.

The Sumatrans found a very different type of buffalo. They took a young bull calf from its mother. Then they put it in a pen all by itself and attached sharp iron points to its horns.

The little calf cried from hunger. The Sumatrans did not feed it, nor did they let it get near its mother to drink her milk. They kept the buffalo calf penned up without food for three days.

Soon the rajah of Java arrived in western Sumatra with his men and his fierce buffalo.

"Release your fighter!" he yelled. "Let us get on with the battle of the buffalo."

The rajah's soldiers let the fierce buffalo loose at one end of a long field. Then they watched as the Sumatrans released the hungry little calf.

The rajah and his men laughed out loud when they saw the little buffalo.

"This will be over in a few seconds," the rajah said. "These fools brought me all the way from Java to take part in this. These people are even more stupid than I thought they were."

The little buffalo calf stood on its shaky legs at one end of the field. On the other end, the rajah's buffalo looked as though it was about to breathe fire.

The calf stared at the larger buffalo, thinking it looked very much like his mother. He began to run toward the fierce buffalo because he wanted some of his mother's milk. However, the rajah's buffalo just stood there, as though he was waiting for his real enemy.

As the little calf reached the larger buffalo, he seemed sure that this beast was his mother. He was very hungry. Quickly he lifted his head to find milk on the underside of the buffalo.

The sharp iron points on the little buffalo's horns ripped into the buffalo's stomach. After letting out a great cry, the large buffalo fell over dead.

The Sumatrans cheered at their victory. The rajah grumbled that he had been tricked.

Since the rajah had lost the contest, he gathered his army and traveled back to Java. He never again bothered the people of western Sumatra.

Since the time of that battle, the people of western Sumatra have built their roofs to look like the horns of a buffalo. Today, they call their land Minangkabau, which means "the triumph of the buffalo."

1. *Why were the people of western Sumatra afraid of going into battle against the rajah of Java?*
2. *What plan did the old man have to save his land?*
3. *What did the western Sumatrans do to the tips of the little buffalo's horns?*

The Perfect Friendship

In this story from Laos, two boys, each with a certain handicap, learn that cooperation can be very important.

Long ago two boys lived near each other in a small village. One boy was blind. The other boy was born with his legs joined together at the knees.

The blind boy grew strong and tall. He was sad that he could not see. He stayed inside most of the time because he was afraid of the outdoors.

The other boy stayed inside, too. His weak legs could not carry him very far before he grew too tired to go on. Day after day the boy thought about his blind neighbor.

"What must it be like never to see all the beautiful things in the world?" he wondered.

The more he thought about his blind friend, the sadder the boy became. He decided to practice walking, a little bit each day, until he got stronger.

One day the boy was strong enough and visited his blind friend.

"You haven't been here for a very long

time," the blind boy said to his friend.

"I have wanted to come," the other boy replied. "You know it's hard for me to get where I want to go. I get tired walking, even after a short time."

"If I could just see," the blind boy said, "I would walk for many miles and never get tired."

The two boys sat quietly for a while, wishing that they were able to live like other boys. Although they felt very different from each other, they felt much the same, too.

"If only I could see," the blind boy grumbled.

"If only I could walk right," the other boy complained.

Then the blind boy had an idea.

"Could I carry you?" he asked.

"If you could, then I could see for both of us," the other boy replied. "You could walk for both of us!"

"Let's try it," the blind boy added.

He crouched down low. Then he carefully helped his friend climb onto his shoulders. When the blind boy stood up, the other boy directed him where to go.

The two boys had a wonderful time. Neither of them had ever run before. Now they ran so fast that the wind blew their hair all around.

"Your hair looks silly!" said the boy, looking down at his friend.

"Does it?" the blind boy asked. "I don't mind looking silly. I'm having so much fun! I'm running out of breath. I have never run out of breath before!"

"I have never seen the sky look so blue," the boy said.

They then stopped to take a drink from a little brook.

"Tell me what the blue sky looks like," the blind boy asked.

"Well, let me think," his friend said as he looked upward. Then, however, his attention was caught by something else. "I see a big bird's nest in that tree," he said.

"Where?" the blind boy asked.

"Up at the top," the other boy replied. "Can't you see it?"

Then the boy remembered his friend's blindness. "I'm sorry," he said, "I forgot."

"It's all right," the blind boy said. "Since you can see it, why don't you climb up and get it? That nest may have eggs in it. I don't know about you, but I'm hungry!"

"I can't climb a tree," the other boy said.

The blind boy had forgotten about his friend's legs.

"I know what," the boy said to his blind friend. "You can climb the tree because your legs are fine. I'll tell you where to climb."

The blind boy felt around for the tree. Then he began to climb.

"That's good," said his friend. "Go up a little bit farther. Now lean forward to the right."

"Here?" the blind boy asked.

"Yes," his friend said. "Now reach into the nest for an egg. Be careful not to break it."

The blind boy reached into the nest and put his hand on something.

"I've got it," he said. "No, wait. I think I've got the bird instead!"

Then the blind boy held out his hand. From below his friend could see that he wasn't holding a bird. He was holding the head of a snake.

The boy didn't want to frighten his friend. "Now hold it far away from your body," he warned.

Suddenly the snake coiled around the blind boy's arm and then spat into his eyes. At that moment, the boy began to see.

Seeing that he was holding a snake, the

An unknown surprise

blind boy screamed and dropped the snake to the ground.

Down below, his friend jumped as the snake landed on his legs. Suddenly his joined legs split apart from each other. Then the boy ran away from the snake.

The snake, just as frightened as the boys, slithered off into the forest.

The boy in the tree climbed down to his friend. The two boys laughed happily and hugged each other. Both of them were thankful to be able to see and to walk.

1. *Why did one of the boys have trouble walking?*
2. *What did the blind boy put his hand on in the nest?*
3. *How did the blind boy get back his sight?*

The King's Shell

Tales that teach the value of honesty and hard work are common in Southeast Asia. In this story from Thailand, a simple peasant boy attracts the attention of a king.

A poor orphan boy named Makato worked very hard at many jobs. Throughout his village, this twelve-year old boy was known for his hard work.

One day Makato left his village and set out to see the world. He wanted to meet Pra Ruang, a king known for his kindness.

After a long journey, Makato came to a village in the kingdom of Sukhothai. He saw an old woman with a water pot on her head.

"May I have a drink of your water?" he asked. "I am very thirsty."

"Who are you?" the woman asked. "Where is your family? Where did you come from?" The woman poured him a drink of water from her pot.

"I have no family," Makato replied. "I come from the faraway land of Mon. Thank you for the drink."

"Why would a boy so young come here all

by himself?" the woman asked.

"I have come to see Pra Ruang of Sukhothai," Makato said. "I have heard that he is a very kind and fair king."

"Is that what you have heard?" the woman asked. "Well, come along with me. Someday you might see Pra Ruang."

Makato was happy to go with the kind woman. She gave him a place to sleep and some food to eat. He knew that he would like working for her. Perhaps one day he would be able to see the king.

The old woman's husband was Pra Ruang's elephant keeper. Makato helped him feed the elephants and clean out their pens. He worked very hard. The woman and the elephant keeper became very fond of Makato.

One day, as Makato worked in the elephant sheds, a tall man in fine clothes came inside. It was the king, Pra Ruang.

Makato bowed low before the king. He was very nervous.

"Who is this boy?" the king asked the elephant keeper.

"He is an orphan from the city of Mon," the elephant keeper replied. "He came here with hopes of seeing you, Your Majesty."

"Is that so?" the king said. "Well, he is a

hard-working boy. Be good to him."

As the king left the shed, Makato saw a tiny shell where the king had been standing. Makato knew that in Sukhothai this kind of shell was used for money. He ran after the king to return the shell.

"You are an honest boy," the king said. "You may keep the shell."

Makato was pleased, even though he knew that one shell wasn't worth very much. Still, he thought he could use it to earn more money.

Makato ran off to the market where different kinds of seeds were sold. He found a basket full of lettuce seeds.

"I have always wanted to have a garden of lettuce," he thought. "Yes, I will use my shell to buy lettuce seeds."

"How many lettuce seeds do you want?" the woman tending the market asked.

"I have one shell," he replied.

The woman laughed at him. "That won't buy you many seeds," she said.

Makato thought for a moment. Then he had an idea. "May I dip my finger into this pile of seeds?" Makato asked. "Then I'll take only the seeds that stick to my finger."

"All right," the woman agreed. "You may

dip your finger into the seeds."

Makato gave the woman his tiny shell. Then he wet his finger and dipped it into the pile of seeds. When he pulled his finger out, it was covered with seeds. He shook them off his finger into his other hand. Then he thanked the woman and went on his way.

Makato planted the seeds that afternoon. He watered the seeds every day. Within two weeks many young plants had sprung up from the ground. More and more plants appeared until one day Makato had a garden thick with lettuce.

"I want to give the king some of my fine lettuce," Makato thought.

The next day Pra Ruang came back to the elephant shed. Makato knelt down and presented a big basket of lettuce to the king.

"Where did you get this lettuce?" the king asked.

"I grew it from the shell you gave me, Your Majesty," Makato replied.

"From a shell? How?" the king asked.

When Makato told the king his story, the king was impressed with his cleverness and hard work. He was so pleased that he gave Makato a job in his palace.

As Makato grew up, he served the king

well. The king trusted him completely.

One day Pra Ruang gave Makato the name Khun Wang. This title meant that he was the most important person in the king's court. Soon after, the king made him the ruler of Mon, his own homeland.

Makato, who had once been a poor orphan, had learned the importance of honesty and hard work.

1. *Why did Makato go to the kingdom of Sukhothai?*
2. *How did Makato get the shell?*
3. *How did Makato get so many lettuce seeds at the market?*

A Father, a Son, and a Donkey

Too many ideas about how to get a job done can sometimes lead to confusion. This Cambodian story tells about a father and a son who let other people tell them what to do.

A man named Chow Khok had a fat donkey. One day he spoke to his son about the donkey.

"Our donkey is very fat," the man said to his son. "I think it is time for us to sell him at the market. If we walk him all the way to the village, though, he will grow very thin. Then no one will want to buy him. So we must carry him."

The father and his son tied the donkey's legs to a long bamboo pole. Then each placed an end of the pole on his shoulder, and they started walking to the village market.

The pair walked along with the little donkey hanging upside down on the pole between them. A crowd of people gathered and laughed at the father and his son.

"Hey, you two," one man yelled from the crowd. "You are very foolish to carry a donkey like that. Why don't one of you get on

Father and son begin their journey

the donkey's back and ride him?"

Chow Khok and his son became embarrassed by the people's laughter.

"I suppose this does look pretty silly," the father said to his son. "Let's untie the donkey. Then you can ride him, and I will walk along beside you."

They untied the donkey. The son rode the animal while his father walked.

Soon the father and son came to another crowd of people.

"Hey, boy!" said one man in the crowd. "What kind of son are you to ride that donkey while your poor old father walks?"

The son was embarrassed. He hadn't thought about his father's tired old legs. He got down off the donkey and insisted that his father get on instead.

The father and son continued on their way. The father rode the donkey while his son walked.

After a short while, they stopped at a well. They were thirsty, and they wanted to get water for their donkey.

There was a group of people standing near the well.

"Old man," a young girl said. "You look like an old monkey riding that fine donkey.

Why don't you let your handsome son ride it instead?"

"Father, what should we do now?" the boy asked.

"I'm confused," the father replied. "First we carried the donkey, and people laughed. Then you rode it, and people scorned you. Then I rode it, and people scorned me. Why don't we both ride it?"

The father and son gave the donkey a drink of water and took drinks themselves. Then the two mounted the donkey and rode on. As they came to a village, a police officer stopped them.

"Why are the two of you riding that little donkey?" the officer asked. "He is barely grown. Surely you will break his back. You should carry him!"

Once again, Chow Khok and his son tied the donkey's legs to the bamboo pole. Then they carried the donkey between their shoulders. They walked across a field to the distant riverbank.

Soon a farmer stopped them. "This field is full of thorns," the farmer warned. "Your legs will soon be cut and bleeding. Why don't you ride that donkey through this field?"

The farmer and his son looked at each

other and shook their heads in disbelief.

"No matter what we do, we cannot please everyone we meet," said Chow Khok. "What should we do now?"

No one remembers what Chow Khok and his son ever did from that point on.

1. *Why did Chow Khok and his son carry the donkey at the beginning of the story?*

2. *Why did the people say the son should not ride the donkey?*

3. *Why did the father and son keep changing the way they traveled?*

Promises

This tale is from Cambodia. It shows that people can get into trouble when they make promises because they need help.

Once there was a man who made baskets out of palm leaves. Each day he climbed to the top of tall trees to gather new leaves for his baskets.

One day while at the top of a tree, the man started to daydream. He thought of what it might be like to own a grand palace that was full of servants. Then he thought that if he were rich, he might have to protect his palace from enemies. The man began to kick at these invisible enemies.

As the man was kicking, he lost his balance and fell out of the tree. He caught himself on some branches, but he was still very high off the ground. The man shouted for help.

Just then a man rode by on the back of an elephant. He looked up and saw the basket maker hanging from the tree.

"Please get me down from here," yelled the

man in the tree. "If you do, I promise to be your servant forever."

The other man steered the elephant over to the tree. He was eager to have the basket maker as his servant.

When the man on the elephant was under the basket maker, he found that he couldn't quite reach him. So he jumped up and caught the man's feet. His forceful jump, however, scared the elephant. It ran off, leaving its rider hanging from the feet of the basket maker.

Now both men were hanging from the tree. They shouted for help until four bald men walked up to the tree.

"Save us!" yelled the two men. "If you do, we promise to be your servants forever."

The four bald men were overjoyed to think that they could have two servants for so little effort. One of the men pulled a net out of his bag. Then the four men stretched the net beneath the two hanging men.

"Now let go!" one of the bald men yelled to the basket maker.

The basket maker let go, and the two men fell into the net.

When the two men hit the net, they hit it with great force. The four bald men were

Men in need of help

knocked together. Their bald heads cracked against one another. Then the four men fell to the ground.

The basket maker and the elephant rider got up, brushed themselves off, and laughed. They were happy to be safe on the ground at last. They became friends for life. Neither of them became the servant of the other or of anyone else.

1. *What made the basket maker fall out of the tree?*
2. *How did the elephant rider end up hanging from the tree?*
3. *Why did the bald men agree to help?*

The Emperor's Magic Bow

Many years ago, the country we now know as Vietnam was called Au Lac. The people of Au Lac lived in constant fear of invasion by the Chinese. The following story grew out of the struggle between the Chinese and the people of Au Lac.

The emperor An Duong Vuong decided to build a great stone wall on the north side of Au Lac. He thought that such a wall would help protect his country from invasion by the Chinese army.

Crews of peasants worked for many months to build the great wall. When the wall was half built, though, it fell over.

The peasants tried again and again. However, each time that the wall would get half finished, the stones would come loose, and the wall would collapse.

The emperor of Au Lac asked the gods for advice. Shortly after he began to pray, Kim Qui, a golden turtle, appeared.

Kim Qui told the emperor how he should have the wall built so that it would stand. Then she gave him one of her golden claws.

"Make yourself a new bow, too," the turtle said. "Put my golden claw at the top of it. With this weapon, you will have magic powers. No enemy can survive the arrows you shoot with this bow."

The workers built the wall one more time. This time they followed the advice of the golden turtle. The wall stayed up.

The emperor made a new bow for himself and put the golden claw at the top. When the Chinese army attacked, the wall protected the battling soldiers. The emperor stood with his troops. Every time he shot an arrow from the magic bow, thousands of enemy soldiers were killed.

The Chinese soldiers were soon driven away. Once again the people of Au Lac lived in peace.

Then the defeated Chinese general sent his son, Trong Thuy, to make peace with the emperor. The general hoped that his son might marry the emperor's daughter, My Chau. The general believed that the marrige would unite the two countries.

The handsome Trong Thuy soon won the hand of My Chau. Then China and Au Lac declared peace with each other.

Shortly after they were married, Trong

The emperor and his magic bow

Thuy asked My Chau how her father had defeated his father's army. My Chau told him the story of the golden turtle and her father's magic bow.

Trong Thuy thought that he would like to get the magic bow for his father. So Trong Thuy built a bow that looked just like the emperor's bow. One night he sneaked into the emperor's chambers and switched his bow with the emperor's magic bow.

Later, Trong Thuy got permission from the emperor to return to China to visit his sick father. His father, however, wasn't really sick at all. Trong Thuy just wanted to take the magic bow back to his homeland.

My Chau asked her husband if she could go along with him, but he would not let her. Trong Thuy warned her that if a new war began, she should find a safe hiding place.

"I will wear my goose-feather coat," My Chau said. "I will drop a trail of feathers on my way to my hiding place. Then you will be able to find me."

Soon Trong Thuy arrived in China. He told his father, the general, the story of the emperor's magic bow. Then, much to the general's surprise, Trong Thuy handed him that very bow.

The general now had the power to defeat
Au Lac. He once again marched his troops to
the north wall of Au Lac. The emperor An
Duong Vuong soon heard of the new attack.
He picked up the fake bow, thinking it was
the real one. Then he rode off to the wall
with his troops.

When the emperor arrived at the wall, he
shot arrow after arrow at the Chinese
enemies. He didn't hit a single soldier.
Meanwhile, the Chinese general was killing
the soldiers of Au Lac by the thousands. As
the Chinese army began to climb over the
wall, the emperor rode back to the palace to
rescue his daughter.

The Chinese army was following close
behind the emperor. He reached his daughter
and pulled her onto his saddle. They rode
down a little mountain path and soon found
that they were trapped. High cliffs were in
front of them, and the enemy was behind
them. The emperor looked toward the sky.

"Kim Qui! Kim Qui!" wailed the Emperor.
"Is this how I am to die?"

"Your enemy is not the Chinese general,"
the voice of Kim Qui, the golden turtle, said.
"Your enemy is the one who sits behind you."

Then the emperor turned his head, looked

at his daughter, and saw the trail of goose feathers. He realized that his own daughter had betrayed him. The emperor got down from his horse, drew his sword, and killed his daughter. Then he jumped from a high cliff into the sea below.

Trong Thuy had followed the Chinese troops over the wall and into the heart of Au Lac. When he neared the emperor's palace, he found the trail of goose feathers. Then Trong Thuy followed the trail to the mountain cliff, where he found the body of his beloved wife, My Chau.

"Why?" he cried to himself. "Why did I let my desire for more power do this to my beloved wife?"

Trong Thuy wrapped My Chau in his cloak and lifted her into his arms. Then, very sad and ashamed, he jumped from the cliff into the sea below.

1. *What kept happening to the great wall?*
2. *Why did the Chinese general send his son to Au Lac?*
3. *After the Chinese army climbed over the great wall into Au Lac, how did Trong Thuy find My Chau?*

The Magic Ruby

In this story from Vietnam, you will read about magical stones and talking creatures that help people. The story also tells us why crabs are always digging in the sand.

Once there was a hunter named Khan who knew all of the animals in the forest. Late one night as Khan sat in his hut eating dinner, a black snake came to visit him. That day Khan had done a favor for the snake.

"My dear friend," the snake said. "You have been a good friend, so I would like to give you a magic stone. With it you will be able to understand the language of all the animals and insects in the land."

Then the snake opened his mouth. Out dropped a large red ruby onto the table. The snake slithered out of the hut and into the forest. Khan wrapped the ruby in a cloth and tied it around his neck.

From that time on, Khan heard all that the animals said. He amused himself by listening to the conversations of the insects.

One day while Khan was out hunting, a raven spoke to him. "Khan, don't hunt anymore today," the raven said. "Go to the edge of the forest, where you will find a lame deer. Kill it and eat its meat. However, you must remember to bring me the deer's heart."

Khan agreed. Then he found the deer at the edge of the forest. He killed it, cleaned it, and took the meat back to his hut. In his hurry he forgot to give the heart to the raven.

Soon the raven came after Khan and swooped down on him. He beat Khan with his wings. Then he pecked at his ears and called him names.

The angry Khan shot an arrow at the raven. The arrow, however, didn't hit the bird. Instead, the raven caught it in his claws and flew off, vowing revenge on Khan.

The next day a man was found killed by the same arrow that Khan had shot at the raven. The arrow had Khan's name on it. The raven had killed the man as a way of getting back at Khan for his forgetfulness. Khan said that he hadn't killed the man, but no one believed him.

Khan was brought to court to be tried for murder. He was found guilty and taken off to a dirty cell in a prison.

Khan took out his magic ruby. He listened to the conversation of the ants that crawled across the dirt floor of his cell. These ants were busy carrying food to a hole not very far from his cell.

"We must hurry!" said one busy ant. "There will soon be a great flood, and all the crops will be destroyed."

"Not only that," another ant said, "all the grain in the king's storeroom has been eaten by weevils."

The jailer brought Khan his daily bowl of rice. Khan told the jailer what he had heard the ants saying. Then the jailer told the king, who sent a servant to check on the grain in the storeroom. The servant found that weevils had eaten all the grain.

Soon after, the rains came. After many days the river flooded over its banks onto the farmlands. For miles around, crops were destroyed.

The king called Khan to his chambers. He demanded to know how Khan could tell the future. Khan told him the whole story, including how the raven had caught his arrow.

Khan showed the king the magic ruby. The king himself used the ruby to listen to the chatter of two mice hiding in his chambers. Then the king let Khan go free, but he kept the magic ruby.

The king heard the conversations of all the insects and animals. He grew so fond of listening to them that he did nothing else.

One day the king was riding in a boat on the Mekong River. He was trying to hear what the fish were saying. The king accidentally dropped the ruby into the murky water. He called for the bravest divers in the land, but none of them could find the ruby. Then the king called for Khan's help.

Khan searched for many years along every inch of the river bottom for the ruby. He followed the river all the way to the sea. Then one day he became very ill and died.

Khan had tried very hard to find the ruby. The king asked the gods to let Khan return to life because he had worked so hard. The gods agreed, and Khan came back to life as a tiny white crab.

Today if you go to the seashore, you may see Khan or one of his relatives. They are still digging, searching for that lost ruby.

1. *Who gave Khan the magic ruby?*
2. *Why did the raven become so angry with Khan?*
3. *How did Khan find out that a great flood was about to take place?*

The Golden Butterfly

This Indonesian tale tells what happened to some people who interfered with the course of true love.

Princess Kembang Melati lived in a palace on the bank of a river. Rajah Banjir, the ruler of the rains, lived in a rainbow on the other side of the same river. The rajah could use his own tears to make rivers and streams. Sometimes he used his tears to make floods.

One spring day the rajah noticed the princess weaving cloth at her window. He could hear her singing. He watched her for a long time and fell in love with her. The princess never once looked his way.

As the rajah watched the princess, he wept many tears because she did not notice him. The rajah was very lonely in his rainbow home. The river swelled up, and the winds rushed all around the princess's palace.

The princess heard the winds. She saw the river rising higher and higher and wondered why these things were happening.

She knew nothing of the rajah's love for her.

One day Rajah Banjir turned himself into a golden butterfly. He flew back and forth past the princess's window. She noticed him and opened the window to get a better look at his sparkling wings.

The golden butterfly landed on Princess Kembang Melati's hand. Then the butterfly perched over her right ear.

"Weave your wedding gown, princess, for your bridegroom will come to you very soon," whispered the butterfly. Then he flew out the window.

Nasiman, the wicked son of the princess's nurse, heard what the butterfly had said. He ran to his mother's side.

"Mother," Nasiman said, "tell the princess that I wish to marry her. Although I am not of noble birth, it is she who will be my wife."

His mother was afraid of Nasiman because he was so wicked. She went to the princess and told her of a bridegroom who would be coming to claim her hand.

That night the golden butterfly returned and again whispered in the princess's ear.

"The real bridegroom has sent no word to your nurse," the butterfly said. "Do not marry the wicked Nasiman. Your true

The golden butterfly visits the princess

bridegroom will come in time."

The butterfly flew away. The princess told her nurse that her true bridegroom had not yet sent word for her.

"Please, Princess," moaned the nurse, "you must marry the man I speak of. Otherwise both of us will die."

Since the princess did not want anyone to die, she agreed to consider marriage to the wicked Nasiman.

"Tell this man that I must have seven days to think it over," the princess said to her nurse. "If he waits on the bank of the river, I will send my answer to him."

The nurse told Nasiman, and he agreed. He went to the bank of the river with enough food to last seven days.

That same day Rajah Banjir called a messenger crow to come to him. He gave the crow a letter and a little chest full of trinkets. "Take these to the Princess Kembang Melati," he ordered. "Make sure that you don't lose them along the way."

The crow flew off with the letter and the little chest. She flew to the bank of the river. There the crow met Nasiman, who was hungrily eating a meal of fish.

"May I have a little bite of your fish?" the

crow asked the wicked Nasiman.

"Who are you, bird?" Nasiman asked.

"I am the messenger of Rajah Banjir, ruler of the rains," the crow answered. "He sends me with this letter and this chest for the Princess Kembang Melati."

Nasiman became friendly. "I will give you some of my fish," he said. "Put down that letter and the chest and eat all you wish!"

The crow put down the letter and the chest and began to eat her fill of the fish.

When the crow looked the other way, Nasiman opened the chest and took out the trinkets. He put some spiders and snakes in their place. Then he took the letter and ran to his mother.

"I can't read this letter, Mother," said Nasiman, who had never learned to read. "I guess it says many nice things. I want you to change them into very mean things."

While his mother changed the letter, Nasiman went off and hid the rajah's trinkets. Then he took the letter back to the crow, who was still eating.

When the crow had finished eating the fish, she went to a brook to take a drink. The waters of the brook sang to her.

"Selfish crow," sang the brook, "you broke

your promise to the rajah. Now something very bad is going to happen."

Something bad did happen. The princess met the crow at her window. She knew that the letter and the chest had come from her true bridegroom. As she read the letter, the princess was stunned.

"You are very ugly," the letter read. "The little chest is full of creatures just as foul as you are."

The princess screamed. Then she tore the letter into pieces. Without opening the chest, she threw it out the window to the garden below.

In the evening of that same day, the butterfly came back and flew into the princess's window.

"Dear Princess," the butterfly whispered, "where are the trinkets your bridegroom has sent you?"

The princess swung her hand and hit the butterfly very hard.

"Surely you are only teasing," the butterfly said. "Would you like to see your bridegroom? He will take you to his rainbow home where the sun's rays make wonderful colors. Now, hurry. You must finish your wedding gown."

The princess got even angrier. She hit the butterfly again and again until he flew away in fear of being killed. He went home and changed back into Rajah Banjir.

The rajah was very angry because of the way the princess had treated him. He started a great flood that swelled the river. Soon the palace was drifting down the river, with the princess and her servants inside it.

"It's all my fault," the nurse called out, as the palace floated past the rajah's rainbow home. "I changed your kind words into mean ones. My son Nasiman stole the lovely trinkets."

When the rajah heard the nurse's story, he understood what had happened. He saved the princess from the sinking palace and brought her into his rainbow home. He spoke to the waves. Then they swallowed up the nurse and her wicked son.

Rajah Banjir told the princess that he was the golden butterfly and that he was deeply in love with her.

The princess knew that the rajah was her true love. They married and lived forever after in the rajah's rainbow home on the bank of the river.

1. *Who caused the river to rise and the winds to rush around the princess?*
2. *Why did the nurse help her wicked son?*
3. *How did Nasiman get the letter and the little chest full of trinkets?*

The Fanged Rajah

Some Malaysian tales teach that wickedness may be repaid by wickedness. An animal is often the bearer of this repayment.

Long ago in a country called Kedah, there lived a ruler who had two large pointed teeth. He became known as the fanged rajah. This ruler was very cruel.

All the people in Kedah hated their rajah. Every day someone was arrested for saying bad things about him. The royal prison had grown full of these people. The rajah felt that something had to be done, so he called together his four top advisors.

"I want you to have one prisoner killed each day," the rajah said. "Make this order known throughout all of Kedah. I want my subjects to stop saying these terrible things about me."

"Your Majesty," said the chief advisor, "these people have not stolen property or killed anyone. They have only talked against you. They should not be killed."

"Do as I say," the rajah commanded.

The advisors were afraid of the rajah.

The fanged rajah

Each day they had one of the prisoners killed in the public square. The people in the kingdom became angrier than ever before. However, they were afraid to rise up against the cruel rajah.

Soon the news of the rajah's order reached Kampar the Mighty, who lived high in the mountains. Kampar had magic powers and wanted to teach the rajah a lesson.

Kampar left the mountains and roamed the land. He told everyone he saw that the fanged rajah was mean, cruel, and wicked. In a short time, Kampar was arrested and brought before the angry rajah.

"So you're yet another man who dares to speak against your rajah," he said. "Who do you think you are to say such things?"

"I am a man who knows right from wrong," Kampar replied. "You're a wicked man who should not be the rajah. I will keep saying so as loud as I can."

The rajah became furious. He called together his strongest warriors.

"Take your swords," he told his men. "Kill this man in the cruelest way you can."

"Would you have me killed without a fair trial to prove my guilt?" Kampar asked.

"I am the rajah. You have spoken against

me," the cruel rajah replied. "Your guilt is very clear."

The warriors lined up, preparing to kill Kampar the Mighty.

Suddenly Kampar used his special powers and turned into a huge tiger.

"Kill the tiger!" the rajah yelled. The warriors were too afraid to move.

"Kill the tiger!" the rajah roared again.

The tiger roared even louder than the rajah. The warriors became so frightened that they ran out of the palace.

"Come back and help me!" the rajah begged. His men did not listen.

The tiger moved closer to the rajah, roaring all the while. Then the rajah, too, ran out of the palace. The tiger chased the rajah deep into the jungle.

The next day, Kampar the Mighty, once again a man, returned to his mountain home. The wicked rajah was never heard from again.

1. *Why was the ruler of Kedah called the fanged rajah?*
2. *Why was the prison so full?*
3. *How did Kampar frighten away the soldiers?*

The Wise Princess

Many centuries ago, visitors to Cambodia were impressed with the respect shown to women. Unlike the custom in many other countries of the time, women were highly praised for their knowledge. Many were also given positions of power in government. The following story is about one such strong woman.

The wise and wealthy daughter of a king once lived in Cambodia. She was Princess Amaradevi. Many men, including four grand ministers of the king, wanted to marry her. However, Amaradevi knew that these men wanted only her vast wealth and did not care about her.

For many years, the princess rejected offers of marriage. Then she met Mahoseth. This man admired her wisdom and her beauty. He didn't care at all about her wealth. After a brief courtship, Amaradevi and Mahoseth got married and lived together happily.

The four grand ministers were bitter and resentful because of the marriage. They made up rumors that Mahoseth was disloyal to the king. For a very long time, the king didn't believe the rumors.

Then one day he heard a rumor that Mahoseth was plotting to kill him. He felt he could not ignore this rumor. The king had Mahoseth sent to the jungle, with the order that he never be allowed back in the kingdom.

The four grand ministers were very pleased. Each one thought he had a new chance to win the favor of the wealthy Princess Amaradevi.

Amaradevi knew that the grand ministers still wanted to marry her for her wealth. She also knew that they had plotted against her husband.

Each day Amaradevi paced back and forth in her room. She tried to think of a way to prove Mahoseth's innocence. She also wanted to think of a plan to show the king how evil his grand ministers really were.

Two weeks after Mahoseth was sent away, the first grand minister came to see Amaradevi. She smiled politely as the man proposed marriage.

"I have become rather lonely lately," Amaradevi said. "Perhaps I will decide to marry you. Come back this evening at seven o'clock and we can talk about it again."

The first grand minister was delighted. He bowed and promised to return.

Later that morning, the other three grand ministers visited Amaradevi. Each one told her how much he loved her. Amaradevi smiled politely and asked each of them to come back that evening at a different time. She told the second grand minister to come at eight o'clock. She told the third grand minister to come at nine o'clock. She told the fourth one to come at ten o'clock.

The ministers were pleased that Amaradevi would see them again. Each one thought he was the only one she would see that evening. They were wrong, of course. Amaradevi had a plan that required her seeing all of the ministers.

All morning while Amaradevi had seemed to be listening, she had been thinking of something else. In the evening she would reveal to her father the true intentions of his grand ministers.

Amaradevi was very well-educated. She had studied poetry, music, and art as well as law and science. She was especially talented in engineering. Because of this learning, she would be able to carry out her plan to prove the truth to her father.

Soon after the last grand minister had left, Amaradevi began to plan for the evening visits. She called her servants together. Then she showed them how to dig a large pit under the floor of her small sitting room. Special care had to be taken so that the walls didn't cave in.

Next, Amaradevi had her servants prepare a mixture of rice, mud, and water. When the servants had finished digging the pit, they poured the mixture into it.

Then Amaradevi showed her servants how to build a trapdoor over the pit. The trapdoor was rigged to open with a rope hidden behind some curtains.

When all of the jobs were finished, Amaradevi called for her personal maid. She asked the maid to pile jewels on a table in the small sitting room near the trapdoor. Amaradevi told her maid, "Greet the four grand ministers politely. Then show each of them to the sitting room."

At seven o'clock that evening, the first grand minister arrived. The maid met him at the door, smiled broadly, and brought him to the small sitting room. Amaradevi waited behind the curtains.

The first grand minister couldn't resist the table of glistening jewels. He paced back and forth in front of it. He put his hand out to touch the jewels, then pulled it back again. After looking around in every direction, he grabbed a huge jewel and stuffed it into his pocket.

At that moment Amaradevi pulled on the rope and the trapdoor opened. The first grand minister fell into the sticky mixture below. Then the princess pulled the rope another time, and the trapdoor closed. It closed so tightly that she couldn't even hear the grand minister screaming for help.

One by one the other grand ministers arrived. The maid greeted each of them and showed them to the small sitting room. Each grand minister put a jewel in his pocket. Each of them ended up in the sticky pit below the trapdoor.

Amaradevi went to bed that night in a quite peaceful mood. She knew that proof of the grand ministers' greed and her husband's innocence was soon to be seen.

The next morning Amaradevi's servants pulled the grand ministers out of the pit. The servants tied the hands of the grimy men, and Amaradevi took them to the king.

"Each of your fine grand ministers had wanted to marry me, Father," Amaradevi said. "Instead, I chose to wed my beloved Mahoseth. However, these grand ministers would not accept my decision. They wanted to find a way to share my vast wealth. In order to get what they wanted, they convinced you that my husband was plotting to kill you. Now I wish to show you who the real traitors are."

Then Amaradevi nodded to her maid who reached into the pockets of each of the four grand ministers. She pulled the royal jewels from their muddy pockets and held them up before the king.

The king was furious with his grand ministers. He ordered punishment for the muddy, rice-covered men. They would have to spend the rest of their lives cleaning up after the elephants.

Then the king sent the royal guards to find Mahoseth. They found him deep in the jungle and brought him home to his wife.

Once again Amaradevi and Mahoseth lived together in the king's palace. Later they became rulers of the kingdom. Amaradevi's knowledge and skills were known and admired throughout the land.

Four guilty grand ministers

1. *How did the four grand ministers get Mahoseth sent to the jungle?*
2. *What subjects did Amaradevi's education include?*
3. *What did Amaradevi's servants do to help her reveal the true character of the four grand ministers?*

Love from the Heavens

The people of Laos believed that no problem could defeat any two people joined together by the God of Heaven. This story tells about the strength of this kind of love.

Queen Nang Chanthathevee and King Pha Nya were very sad because no children had been born to them.

One day the king and queen went to the pagoda to pray. The God of Heaven, upon hearing their sad story, decided to grant them their wish.

That same year, the God of Heaven sent a baby boy and a baby girl to Earth. The baby boy was born to the king and the queen and brought great joy to the palace. They named their son Thao Sithon. The king and queen were happy that their prayers had been answered.

At the very same time, in the faraway mountains, the baby girl was born to a poor, hard-working couple. The parents, too, knew that the baby girl was a gift from heaven. They named their child Nang Manorath.

With the passing of each season, the two

children grew strong, happy, and proud.

When the boy grew into a man, the king sent a messenger to find a wife for his son.

The messenger met a hunter who told him of a beautiful girl named Nang Manorath. This girl lived in a far-off mountain village.

The messenger traveled many days until he came to the home of Nang Manorath. The moment he met her, the messenger knew that she was the ideal wife for Thao Sithon. Her parents sadly said good-bye to their daughter. However, they felt that she would know great happiness as the wife of a prince.

The messenger brought Nang Manorath back to Prince Thao Sithon. The young people fell in love instantly. In time, there was a grand marriage.

The husband and wife did not have much time together, though. Soon after the wedding, Prince Thao Sithon was called off to battle. Enemy forces were nearing the kingdom.

As the war raged on, the king and queen grew fearful for their lives. "I will go to a holy man," the queen said, "to find out what we should do. Heaven helped us once. Perhaps it will help us again."

The queen went to a holy man and asked for help.

"The one who has newly come to your palace carries evil," the holy man warned. "She has brought war to your land."

The queen was shocked at what the holy man had told her. "Oh, no," she replied, "it couldn't be Nang Manorath."

"You must free your kingdom of this wicked woman," the holy man warned. "Only if you destroy her will you save your son and your kingdom."

The queen was very much saddened by what she had been told. How could she have her son's wife killed? On the other hand, how could she fail to heed the holy man's warning?

That same night, Nang Manorath had a dream in which a saint from heaven spoke to her from her bedside.

"Wake up, my dear child," the saint whispered. "You must run from this place at once. Go as far away as you can and never come back. If you do not go now, you will surely die."

Nang Manorath woke up, shaking with fear. She fled into the forest outside the palace.

Soon afterward the war ended. Prince Thao Sithon returned to the palace of the king and queen. His happiness at having helped save his country was dashed by his sadness at finding his wife missing.

The queen explained to her son what the holy man had told her.

"How could you have believed those words?" Thao Sithon asked. "There is not a bit of evil in my wife."

The queen said nothing. She felt that the holy man had been right, for when Nang Manorath left, the war did end.

"Where is she?" Thao Sithon demanded. "What have you done with my wife?"

"I do not know what happened to her," his mother answered. "She has been gone since the night the holy man spoke."

"You did not send anyone to find her?" Thao Sithon asked.

"No, I did not," replied the queen.

Thao Sithon ran out of the palace, still dressed as a warrior. He ran all night until he came to the holy man's hut.

"You will never tell such horrible lies again," Thao Sithon said to the holy man. Then Thao Sithon drew his sword and killed the holy man.

Thao Sithon rode on across many lands in search of Nang Manorath. He offered half of his fortune as a reward. No one, however, knew where Nang Manorath was. Year followed year as Thao Sithon continued to look for his beloved Nang Manorath. He climbed mountains and crossed rivers and fierce jungles, vowing never to stop looking for her.

One night Thao Sithon built a fire to warm himself. He prayed to the God of Heaven for help. Then he hummed his wife's favorite song as if the sound of his voice might bring her back.

Thao Sithon stared into the dancing flames of the little fire. As he watched the flames, a halo appeared above them. It grew and grew until it formed a human shape.

"Thao Sithon," the shape whispered to him, "are you my beloved husband from so long ago?"

"Have my prayers been answered?" Thao Sithon replied.

"I believe that my prayers have been answered," said the shape. Then the human-shaped halo turned into the real Nang Manorath.

Thao Sithon and Nang Manorath

returned to rule the kingdom left them by the king and queen. They ruled happily and fairly. They had been joined together by the God of Heaven.

1. *At the beginning of the story, why had the king and queen been so sad?*
2. *Why did Nang Manorath leave the palace?*
3. *How did Thao Sithon's wife come back?*

Pronunciation Guide

Every effort has been made to present native pronunciations of the unusual names in this book. Sometimes experts differed in their opinions, however, or no pronunciation could be found. Also, certain foreign-language sounds were felt to be unpronounceable by today's readers. In these cases, editorial license was exercised in selecting pronunciations.

Key

The letter or letters used to show pronunciation have the following sounds:

a	as in *map* and *glad*
ah	as in *pot* and *cart*
aw	as in *fall* and *lost*
ch	as in *chair* and *child*
e	as in *let* and *care*
ee	as in *feet* and *please*
ey	as in *play* and *face*
g	as in *gold* and *girl*
hy	as in *huge* and *humor*
i	as in *my* and *high*
ih	as in *sit* and *clear*

j	as in *jelly* and *gentle*
k	as in *skill* and *can*
ky	as in *cute*
l	as in *long* and *pull*
my	as in *mule*
ng	as in *sing* and *long*
ny	as in *canyon* and *onion*
o	as in *slow* and *go*
oo	as in *cool* and *move*
ow	as in *cow* and *round*
s	as in *soon* and *cent*
sh	as in *shoe* and *sugar*
th	as in *thin* and *myth*
u	as in *put* and *look*
uh	as in *run* and *up*
y	as in *you* and *yesterday*
z	as in *zoo* and *pairs*

Guide

Capital letters are used to represent stressed syllables. For example, the word *ugly* would be written here as "UHG lee."

Akulaw: uh KOO luh

Amaradevi: uh MAH ruh DEH vee

An Duong Vuong: AHN DOO ahng VOO ahng

Au Lac: OW LAHK

Batara Guru: buh TAH ruh GOO roo

Borneo: BOHR nee o

Chow Khok: CHOW KOHK

Mon: MUHN

Hung Vuong: HUHNG VOO ahng

Java: JAH vuh

Kampar: KAHM pahr

Kedah: KAY duh

Kembang Melati: KEHM bahng meh LAH tee

Khan: KAHN

Khun Wang: KUHN wahng

Kim Qui: KIHM KEE

Lingayen: lihn GAH yehn

Mahoseth: muh HOH sehth

Makato: muh KAT to

Maksil: MAHK sihl

Maliket: mah lih KEHT

Mekong: MEY KAHNG

Mi Nuong: MEE NOO ahng

Minangkabau: mih nahng KAH bow

My Chau: MI CHOW

Nang Chanthathevee: NAHNG CHAHN
thuh THEH vee

Nang Manorath: NAHNG MAH no rahth

Nasiman: NAH sih MAHN

Pha Nya: FAH Nee AH

Pra Ruang: PRAW ROO ahng

Rajah Banjir: RAH juh BAHN jeer

Sukhothai: SUHK hoh TI

Sumatra: soo MAH truh

Tao: TAH uh

Thao Sithon: THAW o Sih THAHN

Tisna Wati: TIHS nuh WAH tee

Trong Thuy: TRAHNG THI